25.50

# What on Earth? Life in a Rain Forest

Dead leaves?

Turn the page and find out.

Published in 2005 in the United States by Children's Press,
an imprint of Scholastic Library Publishing
90 Sherman Turnpike, Danbury, CT 96816

ISBN 0-516-25315-8 (Lib. Bdg.)

A catalog record is available from the Library of Congress.

Printed and bound in China.

**Editor:**              Ronald Coleman
**Senior Art Editor:**   Carolyn Franklin
**DTP Designer:**        Mark Williams

**Picture Credits** Julian Baker: 8, 9; Carolyn Scrace: 1, 2, 3,
4, 6, 7, 8, 9, 13, 14, 16, 18, 19, 20, 21, 22, 23;, Jordi Bas
Casas, NHPA: 10, 11; Jany Sauvanet, NHPA: 12; Kevin
Schafer, NHPA: 15; John Foxx: 13, 29; Digital Vision: 17,
28; DesignEXchange: 20, 24; PhotoDisc: 26; Corbis: 30, 31

Cover © Gary Braasch/Corbis Images

**What on Earth?** playing dead!

Praying mantis          Dead leaf

This praying mantis hopes to fool
its predators by pretending it's a
dead leaf. If you don't look
**good to eat** you probably
won't be eaten!

# What on Earth? Life in a Rain Forest

WRITTEN BY
KATHRYN SENIOR

ILLUSTRATED BY
CAROLYN SCRACE

Guess what this is?

Turn the page and find out!

**children's press®**

A Division of Scholastic Inc.

NEW YORK • TORONTO • LONDON • AUCKLAND • SYDNEY

MEXICO CITY • NEW DELHI • HONG KONG

DANBURY, CONNECTICUT

# Rain Forests

**R**ain forests are areas of dense tropical forest. Without trees there would be no rain forests, and without high rainfall and a hot steady temperature, there would be no trees to form a rain forest. Everything in the rain forest needs the trees. And trees need birds, animals and insects in order to survive.

Red-eyed tree frog

Golden eyelash viper

Heliconid butterfly

Passion flower

Leaf-cutter ant

Poison-arrow frog

Oasis
hummingbird

Glass-wing
butterfly

Postman
butterfly

Tamandua and
its young

Tree
porcupine

Squirrel
monkey

# Where in the World Are Rain Forests?

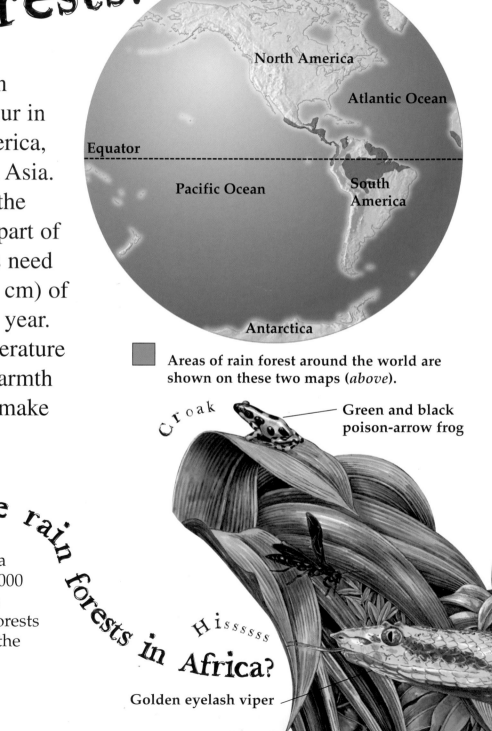

Tropical rain forests occur in South America, Africa and Asia. Most of them lie near the equator, in the hottest part of the world. Rain forests need at least 77 inches (200 cm) of rainfall throughout the year. They also need a temperature of 79°F (26°C). It is warmth and **dampness** that make the trees flourish.

Arctic

North America

Atlantic Ocean

Equator

Pacific Ocean

South America

Antarctica

Areas of rain forest around the world are shown on these two maps (*above*).

Croak

Green and black poison-arrow frog

Hisssss

## How big are the rain forests in Africa?

The rain forest in West Africa and Madagascar covers 380,000 square miles (950,000 square kilometers). These tropical forests are mainly in Zaire, Gabon, the Republic of Congo, and the Central African Republic.

Golden eyelash viper

The largest lowland tropical rain forests are in South America, which is home to over **half** the world's rain forests. Most of these forests are in Brazil, but Bolivia, Colombia, Ecuador, French Guiana, Guyana, Peru, Surinam, Venezuela, and the republics of Central America all have some rain forests too.

## Are all rain forests in the tropics?

Some rain forests are not in the tropics. These are called temperate rain forests. They are found on the Pacific northwest coast of North America, southern Chile, parts of southeastern Australia, and New Zealand. Where different types of rain forest meet, there is no clear boundary to mark the end of one and the beginning of another. They blend and change gradually over a large area.

# What Is the Canopy?

A rain forest canopy, the area at the top of the trees, gets all the sun and rain. From above, the canopy looks like a solid green mass, stretching as far as the eye can see. Some rain forest trees are bigger and taller than trees found anywhere else in the world.

## What is underneath the canopy?

The area under the canopy is called the understory. Many trees in a rain forest have huge roots that help support them as they grow. Below the understory is the forest floor where dead leaves decay along with the remains of any animals. The soil is poor in the rain forest so it is important that everything rots quickly to add nutrients which help the plants grow.

## Why are the leaves so big?

Tropical rain forest trees have really large leaves. They are usually about 8 inches (20 cm) long with very smooth edges which end in a sharp extended tip. This shape helps water run off the leaf easily.

# Jumping kangaroos!

The Goodfellows tree kangaroo travels through Papua New Guinea's rain forests leaping up to 22 feet (seven meters) from one tree to another.

## One giant leap...

# What Lives in the Treetops?

Harpy eagle

Rain forests are full of birds. Parrots are easy to spot because of their bright colors and loud calls. There are over 300 different types of parrot in the rain forests. They feed on seeds, grass, fruit, leaves and plant shoots. They use their strong beaks to **crack** hard shells and to grind their food. They also use their beaks for climbing.

## Sloth-eating eagle?

The harpy eagle is a large bird of prey, almost 39 inches (1 meter) long. It can pull some of the smaller apes and sloths out of trees with its huge claws.

## Killer talons?

A harpy eagle has talons that are 5 inches (12.5 cm) long. They are as big as a grizzly bear's claws!

*Cr0akkkk!*
*cr0akkkk!*

## One of the largest parrots?

**Scarlet macaw**

**Keel-billed toucan**

## Sounds like a frog?

The keel-billed toucan's most obvious feature is its huge bill which is yellow, orange, red, green and black. It has a call which sounds like a frog croaking.

Macaws are one of the largest parrots in the rain forest. They live in Central and South America. They like to nest in holes in trees. Macaws are on the endangered species list because people catch them to sell as pets.

## What on Earth?

## Flying snakes!

Flying snakes live in South and Southeast Asia. They jump from trees, flattening their entire body, and gliding or parachuting to the ground or another tree.

## Don't look up!

# What Mammals Live in Trees?

**M**ammals are animals who are fed on their mother's milk when they are young. Mammals form a large part of the wildlife of the rain forest. Most of them live in the canopy and have special features to help them move easily from tree to tree. Many of the monkeys have **prehensile** tails. This means that their tails are very flexible and sensitive and can curl around and hang onto branches. It's like having an extra arm.

Cotton-topped tamarin

## A tiny monkey?

Tamarins are small monkeys weighing only about 10-16 ounces (500 g). Their main diet consists of insects, ripe fruit, seeds, nectar, and gum that oozes from trees.

## A squirrel monkey?

Squirrel monkeys are quite social animals and live in groups of about 30. Females in the group each have one baby a year, all born around the same time.

## Slothing about?

Sloths (*below*) are so slow moving that they can be in the same tree for years! They live for about 30 years and may never see or walk on the forest floor at all.

## Green sloth?

Algae grows on trees and even on some animals. Sloths can eventually turn a dull green color because of the green algae growing on their fur!

# Is There Poison in the Rain Forest?

The rain forest of South America is home to many different types of poisonous frogs. The frogs are quite small. The largest is no longer than 3 inches (7 cm). Males and females look the same but the males have bigger **toe pads**. Toe pads have great suction power and the frogs use them to cling onto trees and branches.

**Dragonfly**

Skeleton butterfly

## Killer licks?

The frog's poison comes out of the pores of its skin. Even a lick can prove deadly to an unsuspecting animal that tries to eat it. This makes the frogs fearless.

Strawberry poison-arrow frog

Poison-arrow frog tadpoles

Day-flying clearwing moth

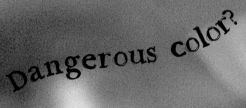

## Dangerous color?

Poison frogs are always brightly colored and can be easily seen by predators. They can be bright green, blue or red with lots of spots or markings. Animals learn to recognize these warning signs and stay away.

## What on Earth?

### The deadliest poison?

One small frog can produce enough deadly venom to load 50 poison-tipped arrows for hunting. (Venom is a poisonous fluid.)

# Are Rain Forests Full of Creepy Crawlies?

Rain forests are crawling with insects. It is almost impossible to count every type of insect but experts guess that there are more than a million different kinds. Scientists believe that one hectare of the South American rain forest will contain almost 50,000 species of insect (including 50 different species of ant).

## What is a hectare?

One hectare is 2.47 acres. It is about half the size of a soccer field.

## Scissor mouths?

Ants are one of the hardest working insects in the rain forest. The leaf-cutter ant cuts up pieces of leaves with its scissor-like mouthparts.

## Leaf or insect?

Many insects look just like their surroundings. The katydid looks just like a leaf.

**Katydid**

**Leaf-cutter ant**

## Too small to see?

Many insect species are too small to see. The hummingbird flower mite is so small it can hitch a ride from flower to flower inside the nostril of a hummingbird.

## Tadpoles in plants?

Water collects in the leaves of plants like bromeliads where tree frogs lay their eggs.

Tadpoles

Bromeliad

Green and black poison-arrow frog

Strawberry poison-arrow frog

19

# What Is the Understory?

The understory is where tall shrubs and small trees grow. The growth of these young trees has been stunted by lack of sunlight. In the damp, dimly lit world of the understory, mosses and algae flourish. They grow on trees, creepers, and even on some animals. Fallen leaves that rot in the cracks of trees provide homes for worms and fungi.

## What is an air plant?

An "air plant" is a plant that grows on another plant. The real name of this plant is an epiphyte. It gets water from raindrops trapped in its leaves, and not through its roots as other plants do. This is why it is called an "air plant."

## Butterflies

Rain forests are home to many different species of butterfly. The rain forest in Costa Rica has over 1,000 separate species.

Ithomid butterfly

Spider monkey with its young

Woolly monkey

Two-toed sloth with its young

Green-winged macaw

Marpesia-marcella butterfly

## What on Earth?

### Howler!

The howler monkey has the **loudest** voice in the rain forest. They can be heard three miles (five kilometers) away!

### Keep that noise down!

# What Lives on the Forest Floor?

Rain forest soil is usually very poor. That means it is unhealthy. The soil on the forest floor gets all its nutrients from "forest litter". This "litter" of fallen trees and leaves, and the remains of any dead creatures, decays rapidly in the damp, warm conditions. The nutrients are quickly taken up into the plants.

The forest floor is an ideal place for many creatures. Ants and termites make nests called "castles" in the crumbly soil.

Deer and other mammals that can not climb feed on the shrubs. Can you spot the ocelot hidden on these pages? (HINT: An ocelot is a kind of cat.)

**Fallen tree trunk**

**Pit viper**

**Strawberry poison-arrow frog sitting on fungus**

**Litter frog**

White-tailed
deer

Cock-of-
the-rock

Ocelot

Slender
lizard

Coatimundi

## What on Earth?

## Does your food come from the rain forest?

Do you eat tomatoes, corn, rice, coconuts, oranges, figs avocados, grapefruits, bananas, mangoes, guavas, chocolate, coffee, vanilla, black pepper, potatoes, cinnamon, ginger, cloves, cashews, brazil nuts, lemons, yams or sugar?

At least 3,000 fruits are found in the rain forest.

# What Is Rain Forest Weather Like?

A tropical rain forest is very hot and very wet. A typical day begins with a cloudless sky and a very light breeze. Even the temperature is pleasant. But during the morning, the temperature begins to rise and the rain forest gets hotter and hotter. It gets so hot, it starts to steam. The steam turns into water vapor which becomes clouds. Around mid-afternoon, there is a stormy downpour that drenches the rain forest. Later in the afternoon, the temperature starts to go down again and the calm conditions of the morning return to the rain forest.

## Walks on water?

The basilisk lizard of the South American rain forests is nicknamed the "Jesus Christ lizard" because it can run on water.

Basilisks have large hind feet with flaps of skin between each toe. These web-like feet help them to run quickly across water.

## What on Earth?

## Flying dragon?

The flying dragon doesn't really fly. It is a lizard found in the tropical forests of South East Asia. On either side of the lizard's body are thin, wing-like folds of skin. By extending its "wings" it glides for distances of up to 30 feet (nine meters) between trees.

# Are Rain Forests in Danger?

Yes, rain forests are in danger. Many countries with rain forests are poor. The governments see the forests as areas where nothing useful grows. They think the land should be used for cattle or to grow crops. But the soil is shallow. If the trees are cut down, the soil will soon wash away. Where will the crops grow then? Even if crops are planted, the soil is so poor that they do not grow well.

## Once a forest?

Much of the African country of Ethiopia was originally tree-covered. Many areas were cleared of trees and suffered soil erosion. Drought and famine hit Ethiopia badly in the 1980s.

## What on Earth?

## How many trees can be cut down in a minute?

About 2,000 rain forest trees are cut down each minute. Mahogany and rosewood are rain forest trees. They are cut down and made into furniture for our homes.

# How would you survive in a rain forest?

People think of rain forests as dangerous places full of wild scary creatures. But really the most scary thing in the rain forest is probably you! You could get lost, fall down a ravine or drink bad water and become ill. If you want to stay fit and healthy stick to paths, boil all drinking water, and leave animals alone. Remember most animals are just like people — if you don't hurt them, they won't hurt you.

## What to take checklist

Remember to take a **machete** so you can hack your way through the undergrowth. Wear sturdy **boots** and thick socks to avoid painful snakebites. Take some **salt** and if a leech tries to suck your blood, sprinkle some on it. Take some **tweezers** so you can remove ticks (small mites) and **antiseptic** cream to cover any wounds. Look out for the gympie gympie tree, it has fine hairs that can sting you — ouch! Remember to take a **hammock** so you can sleep at night without fear of attack by insects and other creatures.

## Rain forest dangers

A **king cobra** has enough venom to kill up to 20 people in a single bite. But it only attacks in self defense or if its eggs are threatened, so if you see one leave it alone.

**Tarantulas** will only attack when they are upset. Their bites can be painful and cause swelling. No one has ever died of a tarantula bite.

A **gorilla** is a gentle and sociable herbivore who will only attack you if you threaten or confront it. Most gorillas become used to humans being around.

## Meat-eating plant?

Flies only, lucky for you — Argh!

The Venus flytrap lures its prey with its sweet smelling nectar. When an insect touches one of the hairs inside its jaws, they snap closed! Its victim is slowly dissolved!

Yum yummm!

# Rain Forest Facts

The Amazon River basin in South America has one fifth of all the fresh water on Earth.

Vast stretches of rain forest are being destroyed. Areas the size of two football fields disappear each second. Over one year the amount of rain forest being lost would cover about 26 million football fields.

Approximately 50 million native people depend directly on tropical forests for shelter and food.

Over 90 different tribes from the Amazon rain forest are thought to have died out during the last 100 years.

On average rain forests have thunderstorms on about 200 days each year. The rest of the time it usually just rains, creating the very humid atmosphere of the tropical rain forest.

Tropical rain forests are so densely packed that rain falling on the canopy can take over ten minutes to reach the ground.

**Red-eyed tree frog**

# Glossary

**algae** simple water plants

**bromeliad** plant of the pineapple family with stiff, leathery leaves

**camouflage** markings or coloring on a creature that help it to blend with its surroundings

**deforestation** the cutting down, burning and removal of forests

**endangered species** plants or animals in danger of disappearing forever (usually because of changes that have taken place in their habitat)

**equator** imaginary line around Earth's widest part

**habitat** the natural home of a plant or animal

**herbivore** an animal that eats only plants

**paralyze** to cause something to lose the power to move

**pollination** exchange of pollen between flowering plants. Without pollination a flower cannot produce fruit and seeds

**prey** creature that is hunted for food

**species** group of plants or animals

**stunted** to stop the proper growth of something

**tropics** hot regions that lie north and south of the equator

**Scarlet macaw**

# What Do You Know About Rain Forests?

1. Where are the "tropics"?

2. What is the area under the canopy called?

3. Which bird can sound like a "croaking" frog?

4. What has a prehensile tail?

5. Where might a sloth live for 30 years?

6. How many poison arrows can be made from one frog's poison?

7. Does a tree frog lay its eggs in a plant?

8. Which monkey has the loudest call in the rain forest?

9. What is "forest litter" in a rain forest?

10. How many trees are being cut down each minute in rain forests around the world?

Go to page 32 for the answers!

Under threat?

# Index

Pictures are shown in **bold** type.

# Answers

1. Tropics are regions around the equator (See page 8)
2. The understory (See page 10)
3. The keel-billed toucan (See page 13)
4. Many monkeys have prehensile tails (See page 14)
5. In the same tree (See page 15)
6. Fifty! (See page 17)
7. Yes (See page 19)
8. The howler monkey. (See page 21)
9. Fallen trees, leaves, dead animals (See page 22)
10. About 2,000 trees a minute (See page 26)

**Yes!** Orangutans live in the rain forests of Indonesia. They belong to the great ape family. These beautiful animals are under threat of extinction. Illegal logging, tree clearance, mining, and hunting are all responsible.